Piano · Vocal · Guitar

2ND EDITION

Love Songs of the '40s

W9-AHS-252

Contents

ISBN 0-7935-4445-9

HAL•LEONARD®
CORPORATION
7777 W. BLUEMOUND RD. P.O. BOX 13819 MILWAUKEE, WI 53213

Visit Hal Leonard Online at
www.halleonard.com

A – YOU'RE ADORABLE

Words and Music by BUDDY KAYE
SIDNEY LIPPMAN and FRED WISE

Moderately

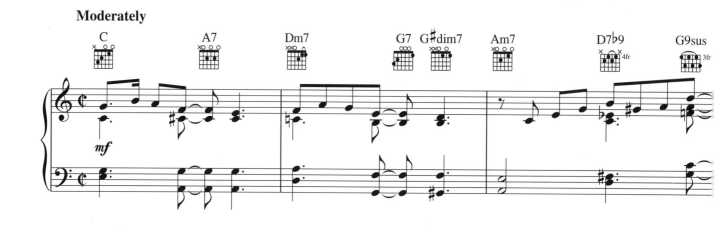

When John-ny Jones was ser-e-nad-ing Mar-y, he

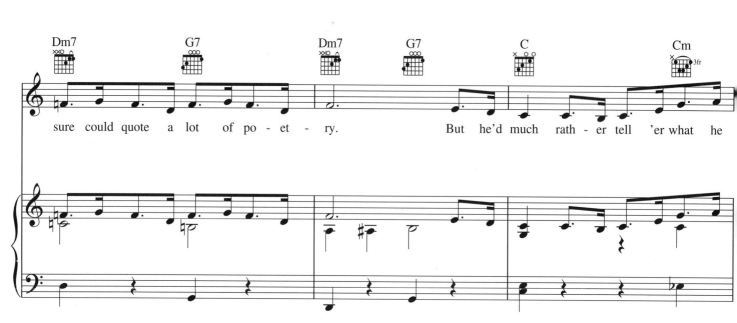

sure could quote a lot of po-et-ry. But he'd much rath-er tell 'er what he

"H," you're so heav - en - ly, "I," you're the one I i - dol - ize.

"J," we're like Jack and Jill, "K," you're so kiss - a - ble, "L," is the love-light in your

eyes. "M," "N," "O," "P,"

I could go on ____ all day. "Q," "R,"

ALL OR NOTHING AT ALL

Words by JACK LAWRENCE
Music by ARTHUR ALTMAN

ANNIVERSARY SONG

By AL JOLSON
and SAUL CHAPLIN

BE CAREFUL, IT'S MY HEART

from HOLIDAY INN

Words and Music by
IRVING BERLIN

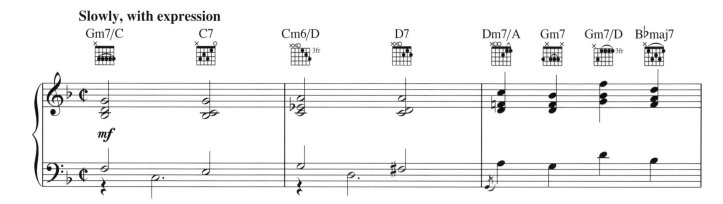

Slowly, with expression

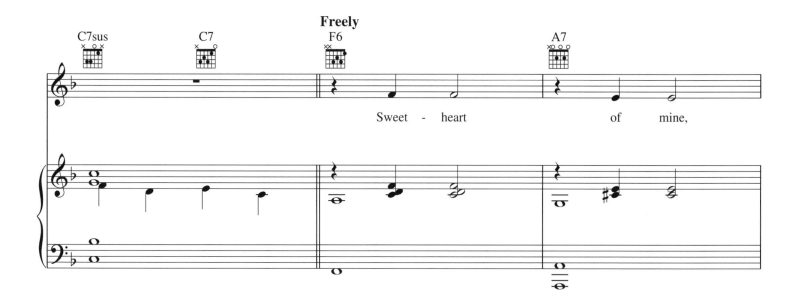

Sweet - heart of mine,

I've sent you a Val - en - tine. Sweet - heart

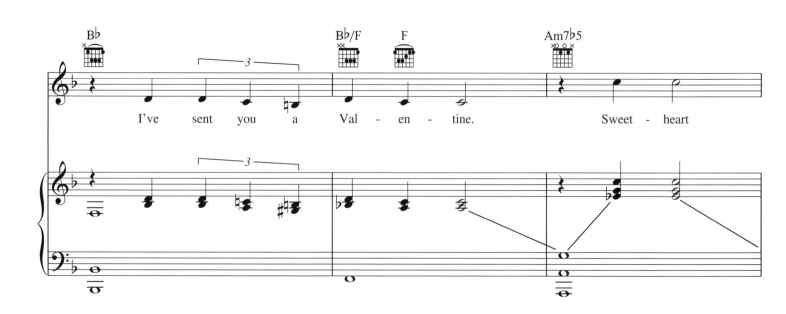

BEWITCHED
from PAL JOEY

Words by LORENZ HART
Music by RICHARD RODGERS

BUT BEAUTIFUL
from ROAD TO RIO

Words by JOHNNY BURKE
Music by JIMMY VAN HEUSEN

CANDY

Words and Music by ALEX KRAMER,
JOAN WHITNEY and MACK DAVID

CLOSE AS PAGES IN A BOOK

from UP IN CENTRAL PARK

Words by DOROTHY FIELDS
Music by SIGMUND ROMBERG

Expressively

We'll be close as pag-es in a book, my love and I. So close we can share a sin-gle look, share ev-'ry sigh. So close that be-

COME RAIN OR COME SHINE
from ST. LOUIS WOMAN

Words by JOHNNY MERCER
Music by HAROLD ARLEN

Slow Blues feel

I'm gon-na love you like no-bod-y's loved you, come rain or come shine.

High as a moun-tain and deep as a riv-er, come

rain or come shine. I guess when you

CRAZY HE CALLS ME

Words and Music by BOB RUSSELL
and CARL SIGMAN

DAY BY DAY

Theme from the Paramount Television Series DAY BY DAY

Words and Music by SAMMY CAHN,
AXEL STORDAHL and PAUL WESTON

DEARLY BELOVED

from YOU WERE NEVER LOVELIER

Music by JEROME KERN
Words by JOHNNY MERCER

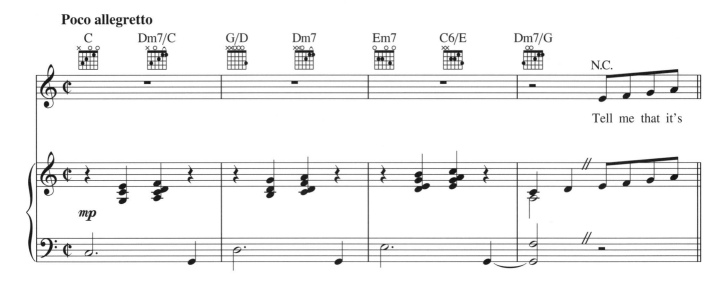

Dear - ly be - lov - ed, how clear - ly I see,

some - where in Heav - en you were fash - ioned for me.

An - gel eyes _____ knew you, _____

an - gel voic - es led me to you; _____

DO NOTHIN' TILL
YOU HEAR FROM ME

Words and Music by DUKE ELLINGTON
and BOB RUSSELL

Moderately slow

EV'RY TIME WE SAY GOODBYE

from SEVEN LIVELY ARTS

Words and Music by
COLE PORTER

(I Love You)
FOR SENTIMENTAL REASONS

Words by DEEK WATSON
Music by WILLIAM BEST

love you_____ for sen-ti-men-tal rea-sons._____

_____ I hope you do be-lieve me;_____ I'll give you my

HAVE I TOLD YOU LATELY THAT I LOVE YOU

Words and Music by
SCOTT WISEMAN

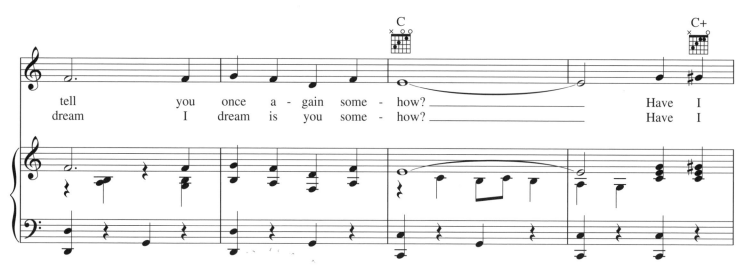

I COULD WRITE A BOOK

from PAL JOEY

Words by LORENZ HART
Music by RICHARD RODGERS

I DON'T WANT TO WALK WITHOUT YOU

from the Paramount Picture SWEATER GIRL

Words by FRANK LOESSER
Music by JULE STYNE

I LOVE YOU
from MEXICAN HAYRIDE

Words and Music by
COLE PORTER

I'LL NEVER SMILE AGAIN

Words and Music by
RUTH LOWE

I'M BEGINNING TO SEE THE LIGHT

Words and Music by DON GEORGE, JOHNNY HODGES,
DUKE ELLINGTON and HARRY JAMES

I'M OLD FASHIONED
from YOU WERE NEVER LOVELIER

Words by JOHNNY MERCER
Music by JEROME KERN

IF I LOVED YOU
from CAROUSEL

Lyrics by OSCAR HAMMERSTEIN II
Music by RICHARD RODGERS

IT COULD HAPPEN TO YOU

from the Paramount Picture AND THE ANGELS SING

Words by JOHNNY BURKE
Music by JAMES VAN HEUSEN

LONG AGO
(And Far Away)
from COVER GIRL

Words by IRA GERSHWIN
Music by JEROME KERN

MY FOOLISH HEART

from MY FOOLISH HEART

Words by NED WASHINGTON
Music by VICTOR YOUNG

Slowly and expressively

The night ____ is like a love-ly tune, be-ware ____ my fool-ish

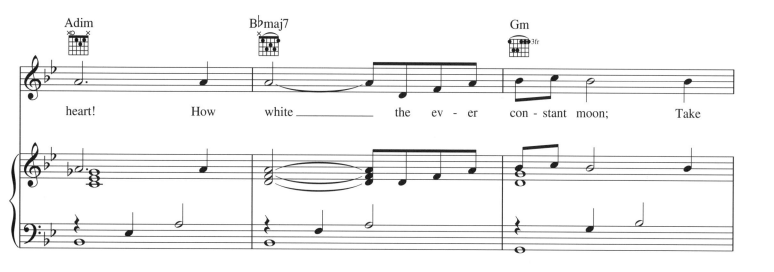

heart! How white ____ the ev-er con-stant moon; Take

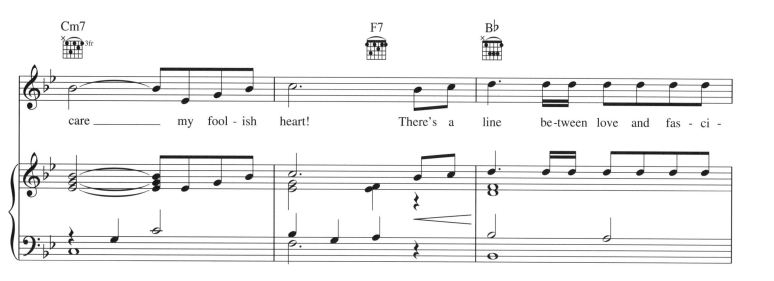

care ____ my fool-ish heart! There's a line be-tween love and fas-ci-

LOVE LETTERS
Theme from the Paramount Picture LOVE LETTERS

Words by EDWARD HEYMAN
Music by VICTOR YOUNG

The sky may be star-less, the night may be moon-less, but deep in my heart there's a glow, _____ for

LOVER MAN
(Oh, Where Can You Be?)

By JIMMY DAVIS,
ROGER RAMIREZ and JIMMY SHERMAN

MOONLIGHT BECOMES YOU

from the Paramount Picture ROAD TO MOROCCO

Words by JOHNNY BURKE
Music by JAMES VAN HEUSEN

THE NEARNESS OF YOU

from the Paramount Picture ROMANCE IN THE DARK

Words by NED WASHINGTON
Music by HOAGY CARMICHAEL

A NIGHTINGALE SANG IN BERKELEY SQUARE

Lyric by ERIC MASCHWITZ
Music by MANNING SHERWIN

Slowly

When true lov-ers meet in May-fair, so the leg-ends tell,

song birds sing, win-ter turns to spring,

ev-'ry wind-ing street in May-fair falls be-neath the spell. I

*Pronounced "Bar-kley"

ON A SLOW BOAT TO CHINA

By FRANK LOESSER

I'd love to get____ you on a slow____ boat to Chi-

-na,____ all to my-self,____ a - lone.____

Get you and keep__ you,____ in your arms__ ev-er-more,__

PEOPLE WILL SAY WE'RE IN LOVE
from OKLAHOMA!

Lyrics by OSCAR HAMMERSTEIN II
Music by RICHARD RODGERS

SO IN LOVE
from KISS ME, KATE

Words and Music by
COLE PORTER

Strange, dear, but true, dear, when I'm close to you, dear,

SEEMS LIKE OLD TIMES

Words and Music by JOHN JACOB LOEB
and CARMEN LOMBARDO

SOME ENCHANTED EVENING

from SOUTH PACIFIC

Lyrics by OSCAR HAMMERSTEIN II
Music by RICHARD RODGERS

Some en-chant-ed eve-ning _____ you may see a stran-ger, _____

_____ you may see a stran-ger _____ a-cross a

A SUNDAY KIND OF LOVE

Words and Music by BARBARA BELLE,
LOUIS PRIMA, ANITA LEONARD and STAN RHODES

THAT OLD BLACK MAGIC
from the Paramount Picture STAR SPANGLED RHYTHM

Words by JOHNNY MERCER
Music by HAROLD ARLEN

Moderately

That old black mag - ic has me in its___ spell.___ That old black___ mag - ic that you weave so___ well.___ Those

THEY SAY IT'S WONDERFUL

from the Stage Production ANNIE GET YOUR GUN

Words and Music by
IRVING BERLIN

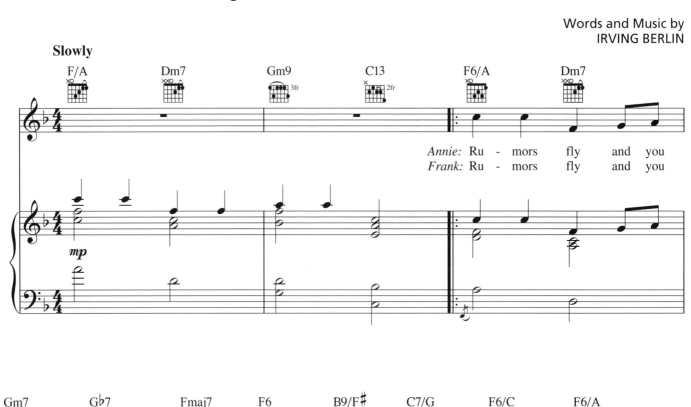

Annie: Ru - mors fly and you
Frank: Ru - mors fly and you

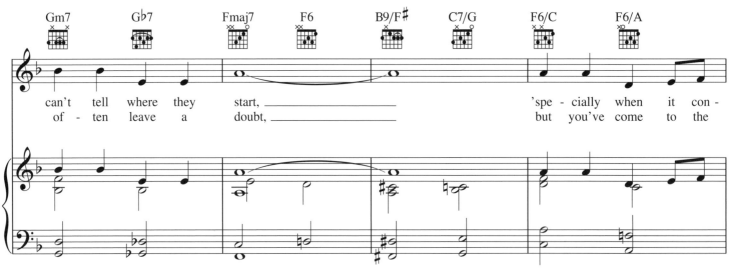

can't tell where they start, _____ 'spe - cially when it con -
of - ten leave a doubt, _____ but you've come to the

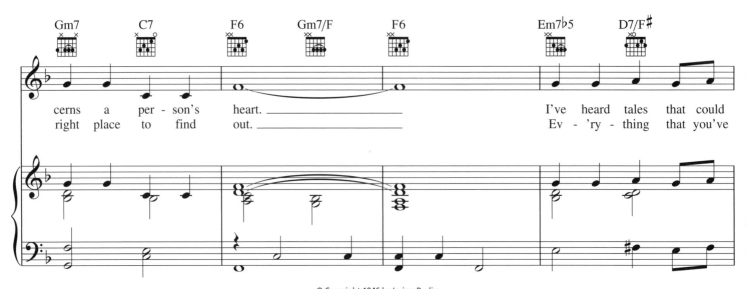

cerns a per - son's heart. _____ I've heard tales that could
right place to find out. _____ Ev - 'ry - thing that you've

THIS LOVE OF MINE

Words and Music by SOL PARKER,
HENRY W. SANICOLA and FRANK SINATRA

YOU'RE NOBODY 'TIL SOMEBODY LOVES YOU

Words and Music by RUSS MORGAN,
LARRY STOCK and JAMES CAVANAUGH

YOUNGER THAN SPRINGTIME

from SOUTH PACIFIC

Lyrics by OSCAR HAMMERSTEIN II
Music by RICHARD RODGERS

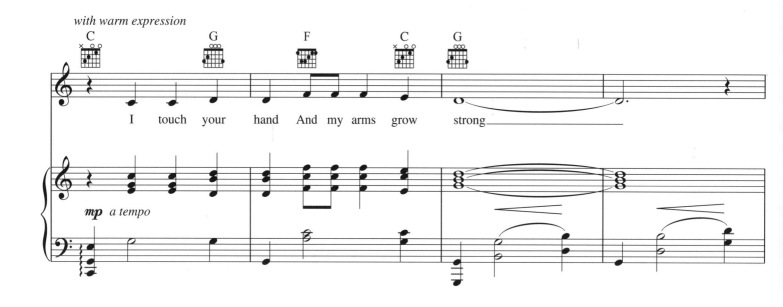

I touch your hand And my arms grow strong_____

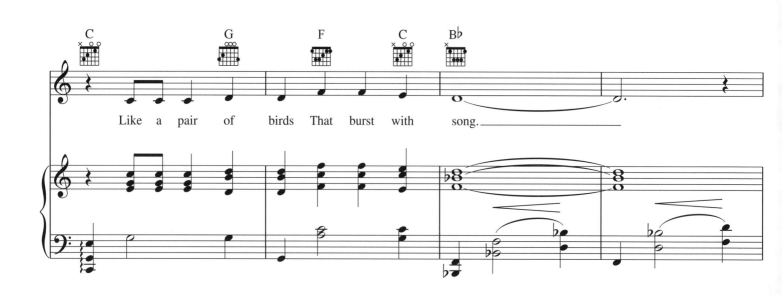

Like a pair of birds That burst with song._____

The Most Romantic Music In The World

Arranged for piano, voice, and guitar

The Best Love Songs Ever - 2nd Edition

This revised edition includes 65 romantic favorites: Always • Beautiful in My Eyes • Can You Feel the Love Tonight • Endless Love • Have I Told You Lately • Misty • Something • Through the Years • Truly • When I Fall in Love • and more.

00359198 ....$19.95

The Big Book of Love Songs - 2nd Edition

80 romantic hits in many musical styles: Always on My Mind • Cherish • Fields of Gold • I Honestly Love You • I'll Be There • Isn't It Romantic? • Lady • My Heart Will Go On • Save the Best for Last • Truly • Wonderful Tonight • and more.

00310784 ....$19.95

The Christian Wedding Songbook

37 songs of love and commitment, including: Bonded Together • Cherish the Treasure • Flesh of My Flesh • Go There with You • Household of Faith • How Beautiful • I Will Be Here • Love Will Be Our Home • Make Us One • Parent's Prayer • This Is the Day • This Very Day • and more.

00310681 ....$16.95

The Bride's Guide to Wedding Music

This great guide is a complete resource for planning wedding music. It includes a thorough article on choosing music for a wedding ceremony, and 65 songs in many different styles to satisfy lots of different tastes. The songs are grouped by categories, including preludes, processionals, recessionals, traditional sacred songs, popular songs, country songs, contemporary Christian songs, Broadway numbers, and new age piano music.

00310615 ....$19.95

Broadway Love Songs

50 romantic favorites from shows such as *Phantom of the Opera, Guys and Dolls, Oklahoma!, South Pacific, Fiddler on the Roof* and more. Songs include: All I Ask of You • Bewitched • I've Grown Accustomed to Her Face • Love Changes Everything • So in Love • Sunrise, Sunset • Unexpected Song • We Kiss in a Shadow • and more.

00311558 ....$15.95

Country Love Songs - 4th Edition

This edition features 34 romantic country favorites: Amazed • Breathe • Could I Have This Dance • Forever and Ever, Amen • I Need You • The Keeper of the Stars • Love Can Build a Bridge • One Boy, One Girl • Stand by Me • This Kiss • Through the Years • Valentine • You Needed Me • more.

00311528 ....$14.95

The Definitive Love Collection - 2nd Edition

100 romantic favorites – all in one convenient collection! Includes: All I Ask of You • Can't Help Falling in Love • Endless Love • The Glory of Love • Have I Told You Lately • Heart and Soul • Lady in Red • Love Me Tender • My Romance • So in Love • Somewhere Out There • Unforgettable • Up Where We Belong • When I Fall in Love • and more!

00311681 ....$24.95

I Will Be Here

Over two dozen romantic selections from top contemporary Christian artists such as Susan Ashton, Avalon, Steven Curtis Chapman, Twila Paris, Sonicflood, and others. Songs include: Answered Prayer • Beautiful in My Eyes • Celebrate You • For Always • Give Me Forever (I Do) • Go There with You • How Beautiful • Love Will Be Our Home • and more.

00306472 ....$17.95

Love Songs
Budget Books Series

74 favorite love songs, including: And I Love Her • Cherish • Crazy • Endless Love • Fields of Gold • I Just Called to Say I Love You • I'll Be There • (You Make Me Feel Like) A Natural Woman • Wonderful Tonight • You Are So Beautiful • and more.

00310834 ....$12.95

The New Complete Wedding Songbook

41 of the most requested and beloved songs for romance and weddings: Anniversary Song • Ave Maria • Canon in D (Pachelbel) • Could I Have This Dance • Endless Love • I Love You Truly • Just the Way You Are • The Lord's Prayer • Through the Years • You Needed Me • Your Song • and more.

00309326 ....$12.95

New Ultimate Love and Wedding Songbook

This whopping songbook features 90 songs of devotion, including: The Anniversary Waltz • Can't Smile Without You • Could I Have This Dance • Endless Love • For All We Know • Forever and Ever, Amen • The Hawaiian Wedding Song • Here, There and Everywhere • I Only Have Eyes for You • Just the Way You Are • Longer • The Lord's Prayer • Love Me Tender • Misty • Somewhere • Sunrise, Sunset • Through the Years • Trumpet Voluntary • Your Song • and more..

00361445 ....$19.95

Romance - Boleros Favoritos

Features 48 Spanish and Latin American favorites: Aquellos Ojos Verdes • Bésame Mucho • El Reloj • Frenes • Inolvidable • La Vida Es Un Sueño • Perfidia • Siempre En Mi Corazón • Solamente Una Vez • more.

00310383 ....$16.95

Soulful Love Songs

Features 35 favorite romantic ballads, including: All My Life • Baby, Come to Me • Being with You • Endless Love • Hero • I Just Called to Say I Love You • I'll Make Love to You • I'm Still in Love with You • Killing Me Softly with His Song • My Cherie Amour • My Eyes Adored You • Oh Girl • On the Wings of Love • Overjoyed • Tonight, I Celebrate My Love • Vision of Love • You Are the Sunshine of My Life • You've Made Me So Very Happy • and more.

00310922 ....$14.95

Selections from
VH1's 100 Greatest Love Songs

Nearly 100 love songs chosen for their emotion. Includes: Always on My Mind • Baby, I Love Your Way • Careless Whisper • Endless Love • How Deep Is Your Love • I Got You Babe • If You Leave Me Now • Love Me Tender • My Heart Will Go On • Unchained Melody • You're Still the One • and dozens more!

00306506 ....$27.95

FOR MORE INFORMATION, SEE YOUR LOCAL MUSIC DEALER, OR WRITE TO:

HAL•LEONARD® CORPORATION

7777 W. BLUEMOUND RD. P.O. BOX 13819 MILWAUKEE, WI 53213

www.halleonard.com

1004